SKUNKS

Jen Green

Grolier
an imprint of
◣SCHOLASTIC

www.scholastic.com/librarypublishing

Published 2008 by Grolier
An imprint of Scholastic Library Publishing
Old Sherman Turnpike, Danbury,
Connecticut 06816

For The Brown Reference Group plc
Project Editor: Jolyon Goddard
Copy-editors: Cécile Landau, Tom Jackson
Picture Researcher: Clare Newman
Designers: Jeni Child, Lynne Ross,
    Sarah Williams
Managing Editor: Bridget Giles

Volume ISBN-13: 978-0-7172-6286-1
Volume ISBN-10: 0-7172-6286-3

**Library of Congress
Cataloging-in-Publication Data**

Nature's children. Set 3.
    p. cm.
  Includes bibliographical references and
index.
  ISBN 13: 978-0-7172-8082-7
  ISBN 10: 0-7172-8082-9
  1. Animals--Encyclopedias, Juvenile. 1.
  Grolier Educational (Firm)
  QL49.N384 2008
  590.3--dc22
                    2007031568

Printed and bound in China

PICTURE CREDITS

Front Cover: **Photolibrary.com**: Michael
De Young.

Back Cover: **Alamy**: Arco Images; **NHPA**:
Thomas Kitchin and Victoria Hurst;
Superstock: Bruce and Jan Lichtenbergen;
Photolibrary.com: Thomas Lazar.

Corbis: John Conrad 26–27, Michael De
Young 13; **FLPA**: Erwin and Peggy Bauer/BCI
38, S., D., and K. Maslowski 29, 33; **Nature
PL**: Jeff Foott 18, Thomas Lazar 10, Tom Vezo
17; **Photolibrary.com**: Erwin and Peggy
Bauer 41, Marty Cordano 30, Daniel Cox 4,
5, 9, 34, Gordon and Cathy Illg 45, Zigmung
Leszczynski 37; **Shutterstock**: Geoffrey
Kuchera 2–3, 6, 22, Holly Kuchera 21; **Still
Pictures**: Wyman Meinzer 14; **Superstock**:
Age Fotostock 42, 46.

Contents

Fact File: Skunks 4

What a Stink! 7

Skunk Relatives 8

Skunks in America 11

Skunk Country 12

Moving About 15

Spots and Stripes 16

Look at Me! 19

That Is a Warning! 20

Ready, Aim, Fire! 23

Enemies of Skunks 24

Anything to Eat? 25

Feature Photo 26-27

Gone Hunting 28

Night and Day 31

Home Sweet Home 32

Fall and Winter 35

Time to Breed 36

Skunk Babies 39

In the Den 40

In Single File 43

New Experiences 44

Leaving Home 47

Friend or Foe? 48

Words to Know 49

Find Out More 51

Index. 52

FACT FILE: Skunks

Class	Mammals (Mammalia)
Order	Carnivores (Carnivora)
Family	Skunk family (Mephitidae)
Genera	4 genera
Species	12 species, including the striped stunk (*Mephitis mephitis*) and the hooded skunk (*M. macroura*)
World distribution	Most skunks live in North and South America; a few species live in Southeast Asia
Habitat	Forests, grasslands, scrublands, farms, and towns
Distinctive physical characteristics	Shiny black fur with a white stripe on the head and back; bushy tail; short legs
Habits	Mainly nocturnal; skunks spray foul-smelling musk when threatened
Diet	Small mammals, birds, reptiles, insects, eggs, grass, leaves, fruit, and berries

Introduction

Skunks are famous for spraying their enemies with a jet of foul-smelling liquid. The stink is so bad that people usually have to throw their clothes away after being sprayed by a skunk!

However, there is more to skunks than just their spray. These striped **mammals** are keen hunters. They are not picky about what they eat and enjoy all kinds of fruits and grasses, as well as meat. Although mostly loners, the females form a strong bond with their offspring and make very strict mothers.

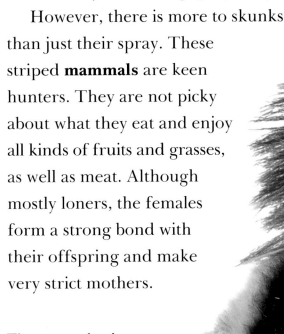

The name *skunk* is a shortened form of a word that means "a foxlike animal that sprays."

5

The spray glands
are positioned
underneath the
skunk's tail.

What a Stink!

The striped skunk's scientific name, *Mephitis mephitis*, means "terrible smell, terrible smell." The animal's spray is like garlic, vinegar, burning sulfur, sewer odor, and sickly perfume all rolled into one!

The skunk's scented spray, or **musk**, is produced by two **glands** in its backside, which work like miniature water pistols. The stink is so powerful it can make people and animals physically sick. It also burns and stings the skin, especially the throat. If the spray gets in the eyes, it can make the victim blind for a little while. The effects do not last long. However, the experience is so awful that animals will keep well away from any other skunks.

Skunk Relatives

When European settlers in America first met skunks, they called them polecats. Polecats are native (European) mammals that look similar to skunks. Some people still call skunks polecats. It is not surprising that skunks get confused with this slender European mammal. For a long time, scientists thought that skunks and polecats both belonged to the same group of mammals—the weasel family. As well as polecats, the weasel family also includes mink, otters, and badgers. Scientists have now decided that skunks are actually different from weasels. The skunks form a separate family, called the Mephitidae— meaning the smelly ones.

Nevertheless, skunks have a similar body shape to weasels, with a small head and long neck. They have a slender body, short legs, and a bushy tail. Like skunks, weasels and polecats can produce a foul-smelling fluid from glands under the tail. But they cannot outstink skunks, the world champions of smelly sprays.

The skunk's thick coat of long hairs makes its body look chunkier than it really is.

Despite their name,
most spotted skunks
have several wavy
white stripes.

Skunks in America

North America is home to no less than four types of skunks. They are the hog-nosed, the hooded, the spotted, and the striped skunks.

Hog-nosed skunks live in the southwestern United States. They are named for their piglike snout, which they use to root in the soil for insects. Hooded skunks live in the deserts of the southwest. They are named after the long hairs that cover the neck and head like a hood. Hooded skunks have the longest tail of any skunk—up to 15 inches (38 cm) long.

Spotted skunks live in parts of southern Canada and much of the United States. These small skunks are skilled tree climbers. Striped skunks are the most common skunks in North America. They are also the largest **species**. Striped skunks are about the size of house cats, but with slightly shorter legs. The smallest skunk is the pygmy spotted skunk of Mexico. It is half the size of the striped skunks.

Skunk Country

Skunks are adaptable animals—they are able to live in all kinds of places, including woodlands, forests, grasslands, and on farms. The hardy creatures also live in dry places such as deserts, on mountain slopes, and even on the tundra.

However, they do not just live in rural areas. Skunks have moved into many city neighborhoods, where they sometimes steal food from trash cans. If you meet a skunk, it is important to treat it with respect. The best thing to do is to back away quietly. Skunks only spray if they feel they have to. These solitary animals would much rather mind their own business and be left alone.

This pet dog knows to leave the skunk alone or it might get a face full of spray.

A skunk lifts its tail out of the water as it wades across a shallow creek.

Moving About

Like many other small mammals, skunks can be very speedy. The striped skunk usually walks with a waddle. But if it needs to, it can gallop along at up to 9 miles (14 km) per hour. However, the skunk has only small lungs, so it cannot keep up that pace for long.

As the skunk scampers along, its slim body moves with a rippling motion. The tail helps it to balance when running and, in the case of spotted skunks, when climbing trees.

Skunks are also good swimmers. When a pond or creek crosses their path, the skunks are perfectly happy to swim across, using a dog-paddle stroke. When the skunk reaches the far bank, it scrambles out and shakes itself dry.

Spots and Stripes

The skunk's coat keeps it warm even on cold winter days. Its fur has two layers, like an overcoat with an inner lining. The outercoat of long, coarse hairs, called **guard hairs,** keeps rain, snow, and wind from reaching the underlayer. The soft, fine fur of the underlayer traps the skunk's body heat, which helps it to stay warm.

All North American skunks have distinctive black-and-white markings. With their spots and wavy stripes, no two spotted skunks have exactly the same markings. Striped skunks may have one broad stripe of white running down their head and back, or several thinner stripes.

The distinctive white markings of the striped skunk run in a broad, cotinuous band from the top of the head, along the back and down to the tip of the tail.

The stripes on a
skunk's back point
to the location of
their spray glands
under the tail.

Look at Me!

Many mammals have brown or mottled markings that blend in with their surroundings. These colors provide **camouflage**, helping the animal to hide from its enemies and also sneak up on its **prey**. Skunks are not camouflaged. Their black-and-white patterns stand out, so the skunk gets noticed.

The bold markings act as a warning to other animals to keep clear, because the skunk is armed and dangerous. Other animals recognize the skunk and give it plenty of room. Many other animals have warning patterns. For example, deadly coral snakes have bands of bright red and yellow around their body. Like the skunk's markings, this pattern sends a warning: "Keep away, or else!"

That Is a Warning!

Skunks do not use their spray without good reason. Their glands only hold about a tablespoon of musk at a time—enough for five or six sprays a week. Therefore, the skunk only uses its weapon in a real emergency.

Most skunks give their enemies plenty of warning before they shoot. If an intruder approaches, the skunk fluffs out its fur and tail to make itself look as big as possible. It hisses and growls, stamps its feet and paws on the ground like a tiny bull. Finally it turns around and waves its tail as a warning. If the enemy has any sense it runs away. You do NOT want to tangle with an irritated skunk!

This bear cub is about to learn a lesson about skunks it will not forget.

The skunk raises its tail before spraying to stop smelly liquid from getting on its fur.

Ready, Aim, Fire!

If the skunk's enemy fails to take the hint, it prepares to fire its secret weapon. A striped skunk arches its back and bends its body into a U-shape so both head and backside face the intruder. A spotted skunk does a handstand on its front feet as it prepares to spray. The scent flies over its head.

Take aim, and fire! Two jets of smelly musk shoot from openings at the base of the tail. Skunks are sharp shooters. They aim for their enemy's face and can hit the target from more than 12 feet (3.7 m) away. That's about the length of a car. As the spray hits the air it breaks into fine droplets that cling to fur and clothing. If there is a breeze, the stink can drift downwind for more than half a mile (0.75 km). The horrible smell lingers in the air for hours.

Enemies of Skunks

With such an effective defense system, it is not surprising that skunks have few enemies. Most hunting animals keep well away. However, a hungry fox or coyote may risk being sprayed for the chance of a meal. Badgers and fishers have also been known to tackle skunks.

A skunk's worst enemy is probably the great horned owl. This large bird swoops down from the branches and snatches skunks before they have a chance to defend themselves. The owls fly almost silently, and the skunks do not hear them coming. The skunk's smelly weapon does not seem to work on attacking owls anyway. The birds do not have a strong sense of smell and do not seem to care whether or not they get sprayed.

Anything to Eat?

Skunks are anything but fussy feeders. They are predators and hunt small mammals such as mice, shrews, voles, and chipmunks. Their main food is insects, such as beetles, grasshoppers, and grubs, which they crunch up with their sharp teeth.

Birds, lizards, and even snakes are also on the menu. Snake and turtle eggs are a favorite meal. Skunks that live near water hunt crayfish, minnows, and frogs.

The skunk is so unfussy about what it eats that it doesn't even care if its prey is alive or dead. Skunks also eat plant foods, such as grasses, leaves, buds, and juicy berries. Crops such as corn and barley are a treat for skunks that live near farms.

A family of red foxes keeps its distance after coming across a skunk in the grass.

Gone Hunting

Skunks rely on their powerful sense of smell when they go hunting. They waddle along with their nose to the ground, sniffing out the insects hiding in the leaves or soil. When a skunk detects a victim, such as a buried grub, it digs it out with its razor-sharp claws. From time to time, the skunk sneezes to clear the dirt from its nose.

Skunks also have very good hearing. They listen out for the tiny rustling sounds made by mice and voles as they creep through the grass. The skunks pounce to trap their prey with teeth or claws. Skunks do not have very good eyesight. They cannot see things in the distance, so this sense is less important to a hungry skunk.

Skunks find most of
their food among leaf
litter—the fallen leaves
that cover the ground.

Skunks are rarely
seen during the day.

Night and Day

The skunk does its hunting under the cover of darkness. It usually spends the day snoozing in its **den**. However if it is hungry, it cuts short its daytime nap and goes hunting at dusk or even on a sunny afternoon.

The skunk's den may be a hollow tree stump, a rocky crevice, a gap in a woodpile, or under a shed. Skunks sometimes take over dens abandoned by other animals. Whatever the nature of the den, the skunk makes a soft, snug nest inside using grass and leaves.

Skunks normally do their hunting alone. However, several skunks sometimes snuggle up in the same den.

Home Sweet Home

Like most hunting animals, a skunk needs a home patch, or territory, to find its food in. It knows all the best spots to look for prey within this familiar area—the little trails that mice use to visit the barn or the stretch of riverbank where turtles lay their eggs.

The size of a skunk's territory depends on the amount of food that is available. If there is plenty of food around, the territory is small. If prey is hard to find, the skunk needs a larger patch to hunt in. Most skunk territories cover an area about the size of two football fields.

The skunk uses its smelly musk to mark the borders of its territory. The territory of a male skunk overlaps with those of several females, so the male can go courting in the breeding season.

This skunk is about to steal eggs from a turkey's nest.

Skunks feast on berries and whatever food they can find in fall so they can grow fat for the winter.

Fall and Winter

In fall, skunks put on a layer of fat that will help them survive the cold weather ahead. In the southern United States, skunks stay active through the mild winters. In northern areas, skunks sleep through the worst weather in their dens.

Skunks do not truly **hibernate** as chipmunks and ground squirrels do. These mammals spend weeks at a time in a deep sleep. Skunks sleep much more lightly. On mild winter nights, skunks leave their dens and go hunting. But when icy winds blow or snow covers the ground, they stay snug in their nests.

Time to Breed

Late February to early March is the **breeding season** in the skunk world. A male leaves his den and wanders through his territory in search of a **mate**. When he picks up a female's trail, he sniffs carefully to check whether she is ready to breed.

The male tracks down the female by her scent. If two males find the same mate, a fierce quarrel breaks out. The rivals hiss and wrestle, lashing out with teeth and claws. However, they rarely spray each other.

Once the pair mates, the male does not wait around. He is soon off looking for another mate. Some males breed with several females each year. A female who has mated often returns to her den for another long nap until the warm weather arrives.

A skunk regularly
rubs musk on to
plants inside its
territory. This
smell lets other
skunks know who
lives in the area.

Baby skunks are raised by their mother only. The father skunk does not help at all.

Skunk Babies

In late April to early May, the female is ready to give birth. She lines her den with fresh grass to make the nest extra cozy. Females usually give birth to five or six young skunks in a **litter**. But scientists know of one female that gave birth to 18 babies—the largest number ever known.

Newborn skunks are helpless at first. They are deaf and blind, and have only very fine hair. However, the traces of black-and-white markings can still be made out in the hair.

A baby skunk weighs about an ounce (28 g) and measures just 4 inches (10 cm) from nose to tail-tip. One or even two of these babies would fit in the palm of an adult person's hand.

In the Den

Some young mammals are on their feet just minutes after birth—not skunks. They spend the first month of life in the den, where they divide their time between sleeping and feeding.

Young skunks are called **kits**. After a week their eyes and ears open and they become more active. By week three the kits are scrambling over one another as they explore the den.

As they wrestle and tumble, the kits lift their tail as if preparing to spray—but nothing happens. Their musk glands have not developed yet. By six or seven weeks the young skunks are able to spray. Now armed with their secret weapon, they are ready to face the world.

Kits enjoy exploring as soon as they leave the nest.

41

A family of kits huddle close after leaving the safety of the den.

In Single File

At seven weeks old, young skunks are bundles of
fine, fluffy fur. At around this age the kits leave
the den for the first time. They do not venture
out alone, but rather form a tight group led by
the mother. She leads the way, and the babies
follow in single file, forming a long line of black-
and-white fluffy balls.

The mother skunk is strict and does not let
her babies stray from the group. If a kit wanders
out of line she may give it a knock or nip. With
all the young in a tight line, the mother is better
able to keep a close eye on her babies and
protect them from harm. The mother skunk
will not hesitate to use her spray to defend
her offspring.

New Experiences

As the young skunks grow, they go on longer outings with their mother. They watch and learn as she traps mice and digs up insects. Before long they are sampling new foods, such as berries and shoots. At about two months old, the kits make the switch from drinking their mother's milk to eating solid food. This time is called **weaning**. Soon the kits are catching their own food.

The half-grown skunks are still playful. As the kits wrestle with their brothers and sisters, their muscles get stronger, and they perfect their hunting skills.

Play-fighting with their brothers and sisters will teach skunks to defend themselves against rivals later in life.

By the age of one,
the skunk will be
fully grown.

46

Leaving Home

At about four months old, the young skunks are becoming practiced hunters. They are finding their own food and sometimes even hunt alone, but they still live with their mother in the den.

Come fall, many skunk families break up. The young skunks wander off to find dens and set up their own territory. Sometimes one or more kits remains with the mother during the winter. But the following spring they, too, set out. By one year old, young skunks might be starting a family of their own.

Skunks do not live very long. But if it is lucky, a skunk will survive to the age of about six, and have many kits of its own.

Friend or Foe?

With their crop-stealing ways and habit of spraying intruders, you might think that farmers dislike skunks. However, farmers see skunks as friends. Skunks eat all the mice and bugs that would otherwise harm farm crops.

Some scientists think that skunks kill more insects than any other mammal. Skunks help gardeners by eating bugs, but they also damage lawns by digging holes.

So the next time you see a skunk just remember, there is a lot more to skunks than just their smell!

Words to Know

Breeding season   The time of the year when animals of the same kind come together to produce young.

Camouflage   Coloring or markings that help an animal to blend in with its surroundings.

Den   The home of an animal such as a skunk, fox, or badger.

Glands   Parts of the body that produce a liquid, such as sweat, musk, or saliva.

Guard hairs   The long, coarse outer hairs that repel snow, rain, and wind.

Hibernate   To enter a deep sleep in winter to save energy when food is scarce.

Kits   Young skunks.

Litter   A group of young that are born to one mother at the same time.

Mammals   Animals that have hair on their body and feed their young on milk.

Mate   To come together to produce young; either of a breeding pair.

Musk   The foul-smelling liquid produced by skunks. Skunks spray their musk when threatened or alarmed.

Prey   An animal that is eaten for food by another animal.

Species   The scientific term for animals of the same type that can breed together.

Weaning   The time when a young mammal moves from a milk diet to solid food.

Find Out More

Books

Nelson, K. L. *Spraying Skunks*. Minneapolis, Minnesota: Lerner Publications, 2003.

Souza, D. M. *Skunks Do More than Stink*. Brookfield, Connecticut: Millbrook Press, 2002.

Web sites

Meeting Skunks
www.hsus.org/wildlife/a_closer_look_at_wildlife/skunks.html
Tons of facts about skunks.

Skunk Facts
animals.nationalgeographic.com/animals/mammals/skunk.html
Facts, pictures, and even the sounds of skunks.

Index

A, B, C

America 8, 11, 16
babies 38, 39
back 16, 17, 18, 23
birth 39
breeding season 32, 36
camouflage 19
claws 28, 36
climbing 11, 15
coat 9, 16

D, E, F

den 31, 35, 36, 39, 40, 42,
    43, 47
ears 40
enemies 5, 19, 20, 23, 24
eyes 40
eyesight 28
feet 20, 23
fighting 36
food 25, 29, 32, 33, 34,
    44, 47
fur 16, 20, 22, 43

G, H

glands 6, 7, 8, 18, 20, 40
growling 20

guard hairs 16
habitats 12
head 8, 11, 16, 17, 23
hearing 28
hibernation 35
hissing 20
hog-nosed skunk 11
hooded skunk 11
hunting 5, 25, 28, 31, 32,
    35, 44, 46

K, L, M

kits 40, 41, 42, 43, 44,
    46, 47
legs 8, 11
length 39
life span 47
litter 39
markings 16, 17, 19, 39
mating 36
milk 44
musk 7, 23, 32, 37, 40

N, P, R

nose 28
paws 20
play-fighting 44, 45

polecat 8
predators 25
prey 19, 28, 32
pygmy spotted skunk 11
running 15

S, T, W

sleep 31, 35, 36, 40
smell 28, 36
sneezing 28
spotted skunk 10, 11, 15,
    16, 23
spraying 5, 6, 7, 12, 13, 20,
    22, 36, 40, 43, 47
striped skunk 7, 11, 16,
    17, 23
swimming 14, 15
tail 6, 8, 11, 14, 15, 17, 18,
    20, 22, 23, 40
teeth 25, 28, 36
territory 32, 36, 37, 47
walking 15
weaning 44
weasels 8
weight 39